MARTYRDOM

Mart

Hallie Fryd | THE COLOR

yrdom

NG BOOK | Julia Gfrörer

Contents

AN IMPRINT OF
ZEST BOOKS

35 Stillman Street, Suite 121, San Francisco, CA 94107 | www.zestbooks.net
Connect with Zest! zestbooks.net/blog | zestbooks.net/contests | twitter.com/zestbooks | facebook.com/BooksWithATwist

Text copyright © 2015 Hallie Fryd | Illustrations copyright © 2015 Julia Gfrörer | All rights reserved. No part of this publication may be reproduced or used in any form or by any means — graphic, electronic, or mechanical, including photocopying, recording, or information storage and retrieval systems — without the written permission of the publisher. | Art / Popular Culture | ISBN: 978-1-942186-06-9 | Design by Adam Grano

Manufactured in the U.S.A. | 4500542168 | DOC 10 9 8 7 6 5 4 3 2 1

Introduction

When I told people I was working on a coloring book about the deaths of Christian martyrs, they would typically laugh. Because who knew that could be a thing! But what could be more serious and more fascinating than faith, suffering, and murder? And these stories don't pull any punches. Ancient and medieval torturers were incredibly creative (who would even think to roast a family in a bronze statue of an ox?), and the martyrs, for their part, managed to resist injury (regenerating body parts abound) in some truly miraculous ways. To top it off, they usually approached their deaths with cheer. I mean, if you were being roasted alive over an open fire, would you joke about it? Would you ask to be turned over so that you could be cooked evenly on both sides? If you can wink at gruesome death as it stares you in the face, then you're made of the same stuff that St. Lawrence was made of. And that is some impressive stuff right there.

Sure, Christianity is the world's biggest religion now, but travel back in time to when Christians were an underclass minority, a marginalized cult that cannily twisted the efforts to squash it into a rallying cry to persevere. How Christians managed to pull off that kind of a guerilla marketing campaign is a complicated question, however, and a deeper one than a coloring book is capable of tackling. Instead, I'd like to take a moment here to address a few other, more basic questions. Questions like…

What's a martyr again?

Originally, the term "martyr" (derived from the Greek for *witness*) was applied to the twelve apostles who knew Jesus in life and bore witness to his philosophy. They were all ultimately murdered for their efforts, and before long, that same term began to be applied to anyone who had died for his or her faith.

Why are martyrs so important?

Martyrdom has been important to Christians from the start. Jesus, after all, was the very first to die for his faith. Stories of martyrs' suffering and sacrifice quickly became a point of pride for the religion's adherents and then a powerful recruiting tool as well. Not surprisingly, the more colorful a martyr's death was, the more inspiring their story became. Strict realism wasn't a requirement either. Adding a dragon, for instance, could really increase a martyr's popularity and influence.

Why not just leave Christians alone?

Early Christians lived almost exclusively within the Roman Empire, and for Romans at the time, the practice of the national pagan religion was an important part of one's civic duty. Nonparticipation was tantamount to treason. Though the Romans conquered plenty of people who worshiped their own gods, those vanquished deities were just folded into the Roman pantheon, and then people went back to worshiping as usual. Christianity, on the other hand, was seen as something new and sinister. Rather than a religion, it was thought of as a "superstition," and its followers were considered atheists. In short, Christians were seen as radical religious cultists who represented a destabilizing force to both the civic and supernatural establishment. Pretty scary, actually.

Who were the most infamous persecutors?

While it might seem from perusing this coloring book that Christians in the first centuries A.D. were subjected to nonstop slaughter, persecutions of Christians were typically sporadic, local, and short-lived — though certainly vicious. There were ten official persecutions of Christians under the Roman Empire, but the bloodiest and most organized were under the Emperors Decius and Diocletian. In 249 Decius rose to the position of emperor after killing the former emperor, Philip (a Christian!). Once installed, Decius promptly launched the seventh persecution. He decided that Christianity had been allowed to become too popular and too much of a threat to the fabric of Roman society, and it needed to be dealt with in an empire-wide fashion. In the beginning of 250, he sent out a decree forcing everyone in the empire to offer a sacrifice to the pagan gods, or provide a certificate (which could be purchased) saying that this sacrifice had already been made. To disobey meant death. Unfortunately for Decius, he himself was murdered just eighteen months later, which put an end to that particular campaign of terror.

The tenth and deadliest persecution of Christians (called the Great Persecution) began around 303 under Emperor Diocletian. Diocletian's motivations for trying to snuff out Christianity aren't fully understood, but he was probably egged on by a subordinate (and Christian-hater) named Galerius. Diocletian released an escalating series of edicts that went from demanding the destruction of churches to calling for the torture and murder of all Christians who refused to recant their faith.

But wow, did these persecutions ever backfire! Instead of giving in and lighting a stick of incense or two as a lip-service tribute to pagan gods, a minority of obstinate Christians opted instead for the iron hooks, wild beasts, boiling oil, and burning stakes of martyrdom. Not only did the Christians refuse to go quietly, the Roman people were actually impressed by the martyrs' passive resistance in the face of such extreme violence and pitied them. The martyrs' bloody shows of faith provided the burgeoning religion with a set of heroic figures to rally around, which helped to increase the popularity and reach of Christianity throughout the region.

Official persecution of Christians by the Roman Empire ended in 313 A.D. with the Edict of Milan, which gave Christians the legal right to practice their religion. However, there have been no shortage of martyrdom opportunities since then either. Churlish fathers, greedy kings, and dubious locals have all participated in the persecution of Christians throughout the religion's history. If you're looking for fantastic tales of suffering and heroism, Christian history is not a bad place to start.

What's fact and what's fiction?

The short answer is: it can be hard to tell. There's the obvious problem that many of these people were murdered over a thousand years ago. It's hard to know anything for sure about anything that happened at that time. Also, because the martyrs were so useful as teaching and recruiting tools, stories about the martyrs' lives were also frequently used to serve those purposes. This explains why so many saints seem to meet their end calmly, if not with outright good cheer; why so many virgins staunchly protect their chastity, even at the cost of torture; and why so many holy men offer hospitality to those who are clearly about to murder them.

Martyrs' histories are recorded in a number of sources. The *Acts of the Martyrs* (*Acta Martyrum*) are the official records of the trials, tortures, and martyrdoms of early Christians. These stories come in a few forms, which range from the fairly historically reliable (court records), to the slightly less reliable (eyewitness accounts), to stories that are either totally made up or based on a tiny kernel of fact. Martyrologies, which also collected the legends of martyrs, were cobbled together from lists of martyrs kept by individual churches and organized by feast day (the same way this coloring book is organized). In the Middle Ages, compilations of the lives of saints and martyrs (most famously in *The Golden Legend)* tended to favor the fantastical over the historical, with a resulting increase in the most outlandish martyrs. Not surprisingly, as the centuries passed, legends changed to meet the fashion of the times. Martyrs went in and out of fashion, and their stories gained and lost embellishment. History, shmistory. More recent martyrs, on the other hand, have fairly clear and often more reliable (if also racist and nationalistic) histories. You'll notice a lack of mythical creatures and last-minute miracles in these accounts.

So, how did you decide what to say about these ancient Christian celebrities?

Like high school, martyrdom is a popularity contest. The surviving legends of these martyrs'

gruesome, miraculous deaths have resonated over the centuries and millennium because they've been honed to their most interesting, and meaningful forms. This coloring book is in no way a reliable history but a chronicle of fifty weird and inspirational lives. In general I tried to read as many versions of each martyr's story as possible and tried to see where they all agreed. Sometimes they hardly agreed at all, in which case I tried to capture the most mainstream version. I'll admit to sharing a medieval delight in the fantastical. And now it's your chance to add your perspective — color these heroic martyrs and their accompanying friendly angels, stabbing lances, pagan idols, pet ravens, and vicious beasts as you see fit! ✳

St. Canute IV, King of Denmark

PLACE OF DEATH	YEAR OF DEATH	MANNER OF DEATH	FEAST DAY
Odense	*1086 A.D.*	*Stabbed in church by revolutionaries*	*January 19*

One of the many illegitimate sons of King Sven Estridsen, Canute (also known as Knud) ascended to the Danish throne in 1081. From the start, he was an ambitious ruler, giving himself all kinds of new powers over his subjects, including the enforced observation of Catholic holidays and a steep (and very unpopular) tax to fund the church's efforts. In another unpopular move, he claimed the English throne as his own, since his great-grand-uncle, Canute the Great, had ruled a united Denmark, Norway, and England until 1035. Canute assembled over one thousand ships in the North Sea for his planned attack, but civil and political unrest at home kept him from joining his fleet for so long that most of the warriors, who were really farmers, had to return home to harvest their crops, thus abandoning the English invasion before it began.

While Canute was waiting waiting for his farmer-warriors to return from harvest so he could regroup his fleet, a mutiny broke out in the town of Vendsyssel, where he was staying. The revolutionaries, enraged by the king's many new taxes and tithes, pursued Canute and his party across Denmark to Odense, where Canute and his people took refuge in a church. Though Canute and his followers may have thought they were protected by the sanctuary of the church, the mob of peasants disagreed. They flooded the church and murdered Canute — most likely with a sword or lance through his leg or stomach — one of his brothers, and seventeen of his followers right in front of the altar. After Canute's death, Denmark suffered a massive crop failure, which many saw as divine retribution for the king's sacrilegious murder. ✠

PATRON SAINT OF: *Denmark*

St. Sebastian

PLACE OF DEATH	YEAR OF DEATH	MANNER OF DEATH	FEAST DAY
Rome	288 A.D.	*Survived a slew of arrows only to be clubbed to death*	*January 20*

According to legend (little about Sebastian's life, besides his death, can be verified), Sebastian managed to hide his Christian faith for years despite serving as an officer of the Imperial Roman Army and captain of the prestigious Praetorian Guard. With the power and respect that came with his posts, he was able to help other Christians without calling a lot of attention to himself. In one episode, Sebastian convinced two brothers, Marcellian and Marcus, to choose their faith, immortal souls, and martyrdom over the wishes of their family, who pled with them to abandon their religion to save their lives. Sebastian also secretly converted a number of high-level Roman officials, including the prefect of Rome, who set his slaves and all the city's prisoners free before resigning to live quietly in the country.

Unlike the prefect, though, most of Sebastian's converts died painful deaths thanks to their new religion, and eventually it became impossible for Sebastian to hide his own Christianity from Emperor Diocletian. Upset that one of his most loyal and trusted soldiers had been traitorously deceiving him, Diocletian sentenced Sebastian to be tied to a pillar and shot through with arrows. Soldiers obediently riddled his body with arrows and left him for dead. But when a local woman came to bury his body later that night, she found him still clinging to life. Happy to find him alive, she brought him home and nursed him back to health. But as soon as he was able, Sebastian returned to the city to berate Diocletian for mistreating Christians and to slander his pagan gods. Diocletian responded by having Sebastian arrested and beaten to death — for good, this time — with stones. In a final indignity, his body was thrown in a public bathroom. Sebastian had the last laugh, however, appearing as a spirit to a widow with instructions on where to find his body and where to bury it.

Sebastian was a favorite of Renaissance painters and is typically shown in art tied nearly naked to a pillar or tree, and pierced with arrows. ✠

PATRON SAINT OF: *athletes; soldiers; archers; plague sufferers*

St. Agnes

PLACE OF DEATH	YEAR OF DEATH	MANNER OF DEATH	FEAST DAY
Rome	304 A.D.	Beheaded in a stadium when she couldn't be burned	January 21

There are many different accounts of the life, degradation, escape, and ultimate death of young Agnes of Rome. None of these stories are believed to be wholly true, but according to most, Agnes was born to a wealthy noble family who raised her to be covertly Catholic. Her troubles started when she reached puberty and began attracting the attention of the city's most eligible bachelors. When confronted with the declaration that the wealthy beauty was already married (to Jesus), one or more of her spurned suitors denounced her to a local judge. The judge first tried to sweet-talk Agnes into abandoning her religion and making a sacrifice to the pagan gods; when that failed, he threatened her with every kind of torture. When she still refused, he ordered she be stripped naked and dragged to a brothel to be raped.

Unafraid, the naked Agnes prayed, causing her hair to grow so long it covered her entire body and protected her virtue. Once at the brothel, most of the men who had gathered to defile her were dumbstruck with awe at the sight of her piety. All but one left feeling sheepish after their encounter with the soon-to-be martyr — sheepish, but edified. The judge's son alone attempted to part her miraculous, dense hair, and instantly he was struck blind (some accounts even say he died after this transgression). Agnes restored his eyesight and/or life, after which he immediately converted to Christianity. Though she retained her precious virginity, Agnes's refusal to abandon her faith meant she was still facing a death sentence. She was first taken to a stadium and tied to a stake to be burned. Once lit, however, the flames parted away from Agnes without touching her. Exasperated, a soldier either stabbed her in the throat or struck off her head with a sword, killing her. Agnes is frequently depicted in art with a lamb as a tribute to her hard-won chastity. ✠

PATRON SAINT OF: *betrothed couples; chastity; girls; rape victims*

St. Meinrad

PLACE OF DEATH	YEAR OF DEATH	MANNER OF DEATH	FEAST DAY
Solgen	*861 A.D.*	*Beaten to death by thieves*	*January 21*

Meinrad was born to a noble family in what is now Switzerland. He joined the Benedictine order and taught for a time in Zurich, but in 828 A.D. he received permission to become a hermit. For seven years he lived in a hut in the Black Forest on the slopes of Mount Etzel, where he (in classic hermit style) adopted and tamed a pair of ravens. He became famous for his holiness and attracted so many pilgrims and students that he had to move farther into the woods to regain some solitude. No matter how deep he went, however, pilgrims still sought him out.

One night, while saying Mass for St. Agnes's (page 14) feast day, he had a vision that that Mass would be his last. As soon as he finished praying, two visitors appeared. Meinrad welcomed and fed them, but they were no pilgrims. They were thieves who had heard about the crowds of pilgrims and assumed Meinrad's hut would be full of valuables. When they realized the hermit had nothing of worth, they beat him to death, despite the ravens that dove and pecked and screeched at them in an attempt to defend their master. The murderers fled the hermit's hut, but the ravens followed, supposedly continuing their attack and drawing enough attention that the murderers were arrested and sentenced to death. According to legend, the ravens even circled above the scaffolding while the two men were hanged. Meinrad is frequently depicted in art as a dead monk with two ravens circling him, or (somewhat less dramatically) as a monk eating fish with a widow. ✠

PATRON SAINT OF: *Einsiedeln, Switzerland; hospitality*

St. Timothy

PLACE OF DEATH	YEAR OF DEATH	MANNER OF DEATH	FEAST DAY
Ephesus	*97 A.D.*	*Beaten and stoned to death by a pagan mob*	*January 26*

Though born to a Greek father, Timothy, along with his mother and grandmother, were converted to Christianity when the apostle Paul passed though their hometown of Lystra (in modern-day Turkey). When Paul came back again a few years later, he found that Timothy had become so well respected as a Christian that Paul took him on as his disciple. Though timid and ill — he suffered from chronic stomach problems — Timothy cheerfully left his family and home behind, apparently eager to travel in poverty and perpetual stomach pain with Paul as a missionary.

Timothy soon became one of Paul's most trusted and valuable disciples. In 64 A.D., Paul left Timothy in Ephesus (also in modern-day Turkey) to serve as a bishop. A year later they had their last goodbye in a Roman prison, where Paul awaited his own martyrdom. Timothy spent the next thirty years in Ephesus, finally meeting his death while trying to disrupt the Dionysian festival of Catagogia, during which pagans marched through town with an idol in one hand and a club in the other. When Timothy, without thinking very far ahead, attempted to halt their procession by insulting their gods and shouting about the righteousness of Christianity, the angry pagans turned on him. They beat him with their clubs and dragged him through the streets before finally stoning him to death. Timothy is frequently depicted in art holding the tools of his demise: a stone and a club. ✠

PATRON SAINT OF: *people suffering from stomach trouble and intestinal disorders*

St. Blaise

PLACE OF DEATH	YEAR OF DEATH	MANNER OF DEATH	FEAST DAY
Sebaste	315 A.D.	Stretched on the rack, torn with hot combs, and beheaded	February 3

Little is known for sure about Blaise (also known as Blasé), but it's believed that he was the bishop of Sebaste, Armenia, and known for his gentle and humble nature. At the beginning of the Diocletian persecution, he fled the city to live as a hermit in a cave in Mount Argaeus. Though technically in hiding, he was sought out and eventually found by the sick, whom he miraculously cured. He also was supposedly visited by wild animals, which seemed to enjoy his company and sometimes brought him food. Ironically, it was his friendly relationship with the animal kingdom that ended up spelling his demise. He was discovered when the new Emperor Licinius Licinianus sent hunters into the woods to capture the wild animals that were used to attack Christians in the arena. Since all the wild animals were gathered peacefully around Blaise's cave, the hermit was found and arrested.

En route to his torture, Blaise continued to work miracles, healing a boy with a fish bone caught in his throat and convincing a wolf to release a poor widow's pig. But he was not granted the same kindness. In prison, Blaise was whipped and his body was torn with hooks. The torture never shook his faith though, and the pagan holy women who were sent to collect his blood to use as a sacrifice to their gods saw this and converted to Christianity themselves. The women were all beheaded, along with their children. After that, Blaise's torture became even more grotesque: he was stretched on the rack, had his flesh torn with hot combs, and was forced to wear a coat of red-hot mail. Eventually, he was taken to a lake to be drowned. Instead of sinking into the water, Blaise sat placidly, and miraculously, on the surface and dared any pagan to try to do the same. Many tried, and all but Blaise drowned. Finally, Blaise heard a voice from heaven commanding him to accept his martyrdom, so he calmly walked back to land and was beheaded. Blaise is typically represented in art as a hermit tending animals, healing a choking boy, or simply holding the iron-wool comb that was used to torture him. ✻

PATRON SAINT OF: *physicians; wild animals; people with throat maladies or neck complaints*

St. John de Britto

PLACE OF DEATH	YEAR OF DEATH	MANNER OF DEATH	FEAST DAY
Oriyur	*1693 A.D.*	*Tortured and beheaded for breaking up a polygamous marriage*	*February 4*

John de Britto was born in Lisbon, Portugal, in 1647 to a rich and powerful family. During a serious childhood illness, he prayed to St. Francis Xavier, and after recovering, he became determined to follow in the famous Jesuit missionary's footsteps. John joined the Jesuits at age fifteen, and eleven years later, ignoring the wishes of family members who even persuaded the Pope to intervene on their behalf, John left on a mission to Madurai, a city in southern India. Once there, John tried to gain the locals' trust by living as they did, learning their language, becoming a vegan, and even joining the noble Brahmin caste. However, not everyone was won over, to say the least. In 1684 while preaching in Maravar, John was taken into custody and tortured for days before being released. Though he survived the ordeal, he was expelled from the country and forced to return to Portugal.

Though King Pedro II and even the Pope urged him to stay in Portugal, John mustered a new company of missionaries and set off again for Maravar. Three years later, he made a fateful convert: a local prince named Thadiyathevan. John explained to the prince that the correct Christian number of wives to have was just one, and he convinced Thadiyathevan to dismiss all but one of his wives. Good for God, bad for the rest of the wives — and unfortunately, one of the discarded wives was the niece of a neighboring king, Sethupathi. Furious on account of his niece's mistreatment, Sethupathi began a campaign of persecution against the Jesuits. John was again captured and tortured, and commanded to stop meddling and to leave the country. When he refused, he was taken to the village of Oriyur and beheaded. ✠

PATRON SAINT OF: *Portugal; the Roman Catholic Diocese of Sivaganga*

St. Agatha

PLACE OF DEATH	YEAR OF DEATH	MANNER OF DEATH	FEAST DAY
Sicily	*251 A.D.*	*Whipped, burned, mutilated, and rolled in hot coals and broken glass*	*February 5*

Though Agatha is one of the most popular virgin martyrs (yes, that's a category), there's little evidence about her life beyond her place of birth and that she was martyred. According to legend, Agatha was born into a wealthy and influential family in Sicily, but as she entered her teenage years, her beauty and her faith started to cause her trouble. Agatha turned down suitor after suitor but had the misfortune of catching the eye of Quintianus, the governor of Sicily. His attempts to seduce her, which included both a marriage proposal and an attempt to force her into prostitution (his definition of "seduction" was apparently quite open-ended), failed: she had pledged her virginity to God.

Furious at Agatha's principled resistance, Quintianus turned to revenge. Luckily for him (and unluckily for Agatha), the Emperor Decius had then just begun a fresh campaign of per-secution against Christians (whose increasing popularity seemed to pose a threat to his pagan faith). Quintianus outed Agatha as a Christian and turned her over to the local magistrate. Refusing to renounce her faith, she was whipped, burnt with hot irons, and pierced at the sides with sharp hooks, all of which she allegedly withstood cheerfully.

Her upbeat attitude in the face of torture angered the magistrate so much that he ordered her breasts either cut off or torn off with pincers (depending on whose account you're reading). According to legend, a vision of the apostle St. Peter visited her in the dungeon, healing her wounds and replacing her breasts. This was only a momentary respite, however. The hard-to-kill virgin was finally rolled naked in hot coals and broken glass, and taken back to her dungeon room to die. St. Agatha is frequently pictured in art holding her severed breasts on a platter or plate. ✠

PATRON SAINT OF: *people suffering from breast cancer and other breast maladies; nurses*

St. Apollonia

PLACE OF DEATH	YEAR OF DEATH	MANNER OF DEATH	FEAST DAY
Alexandria	*249 A.D.*	*Definitely not by suicide (except sort of)*	*February 9*

Apollonia was an elderly, virginal, and well-respected deaconess living in Alexandria, Egypt, at the end of the reign of Philip the Arab. Though Christians in the Roman Empire were left relatively unmolested throughout Philip's reign, things went a little haywire in 249 A.D. during the yearlong festivities celebrating the millennial anniversary of the founding of Rome. One well-known poet and prophet in particular worked hard to stir up resentment and superstition against Christians. The potent combination of the festivities, the poetry, and the prophesies sent mobs of pagans roaming the city, looking for Christians to rob, torture, and murder.

Apollonia was caught by one such mob while fleeing Alexandria. When she refused to renounce her faith, the pagans retaliated with a violent removal of her teeth (some versions say that they were pulled out with pincers, others that they were punched out; quite painful either way). They then built a bonfire and threatened to throw her into it if she didn't either badmouth her god or swear an oath to theirs. As they were about to toss her into the fire, she asked for a moment to think it over — then turned and jumped into the flames to deny them the satisfaction of murdering her. *In your face, pagans!* While to some this kind of martyrdom looks a lot like suicide (which is forbidden in Christianity), it was a popular and accepted way for virgin martyrs to die in order to protect both their faith and their chastity. Apollonia is frequently depicted in art either with pincers holding a tooth or with a necklace decorated with a golden tooth. ✜

PATRON SAINT OF: *dentists; toothache sufferers*

St. Valentine

PLACE OF DEATH	YEAR OF DEATH	MANNER OF DEATH	FEAST DAY
Rome	*270 A.D.*	*Unromantically clubbed and beheaded*	*February 14*

Not much is known about Valentine's early life. In fact, his story may be a combination of those of two or three different Valentines. The prevailing legend around the Valentine who had the romantic holiday named after him claims he was a physician and priest (and possibly bishop) who was arrested for secretly marrying Christian couples and giving assistance to martyrs imprisoned under Claudius II, also known as Claudius the Cruel. While in prison, Valentine restored the vision of his jailor's blind daughter, converting the whole family to Christianity in the process. Despite performing this medical miracle, Valentine still received a fatal sentence. He was stoned and clubbed before he was finally beheaded for refusing to renounce his faith. On the morning of his execution, February 14, he supposedly wrote a farewell message to the jailor's daughter signed, "From your Valentine."

Valentine's name may also have become associated with romance because the date of his martyrdom coincides with the celebration of the Roman holiday Lupercalia. During Lupercalia, young men ran through the city whipping young women with the newly flayed skin of sacrificed animals (which was believed to encourage fertility). Nothing says romance like being slapped with a bloody goatskin! The men also drew from a box the name of an available woman with whom they would be "matched" for the duration of the holiday. Not surprisingly, Valentine is frequently depicted surrounded by roses and birds, performing marriages, refusing to worship an idol, or being beheaded. ✠

PATRON SAINT OF: *young people; love and lovers; happy marriages; beekeepers*

St. Polycarp

PLACE OF DEATH	YEAR OF DEATH	MANNER OF DEATH	FEAST DAY
Rome	*ca. 2nd century A.D.*	*Burned at the stake and stabbed to death*	*February 23*

Polycarp was one of the first disciples of the apostles, who were the first disciples of Jesus. John the Evangelist established Polycarp as the bishop of Smyrna (in modern-day Turkey) when Polycarp was still in his mid-twenties. Polycarp lived there until his late eighties, when a wave of persecution swept through the Roman Empire. Tired of seeing less prestigious Christians eaten by lions in the Coliseum, people cried out for Polycarp's head. Though he claimed not to be afraid of the mob, Polycarp let his friends convince him to hide out in a farmhouse outside of town. Three days before his martyrdom, he had a vision of his pillow catching on fire, which he took as a portent of his own fiery death.

When the soldiers did come for him, Polycarp didn't hide. Instead, he invited them in for dinner and asked for a couple hours in which to pray while they ate. Afterward, he was taken into the city and brought before the tribunal, which tried without success to get him to renounce his Christianity and make a small sacrifice to the pagan gods. After he was found guilty of being an unrepentant Christian, the crowd demanded Polycarp be burned alive, and they piled a huge mound of wood under him. But when the fire caught, it miraculously bellowed out around him, encircling him but not burning him. Instead, his body is said to have let out a fragrant, spicy smell. Angry that their bloodlust had been thwarted, the pagans demanded action. A soldier acquiesced and ran Polycarp through with a spear, creating a geyser of blood so powerful that it supposedly doused the fire instantly. ✟

PATRON SAINT OF: *people suffering from earaches or dysentery; pilgrims*

St. Perpetua and St. Felicity

PLACE OF DEATH	YEAR OF DEATH	MANNER OF DEATH	FEAST DAY
Carthage	*203 A.D.*	*Mauled by a wild heifer, then finished off by a gladiator*	*March 7*

Perpetua and Felicity lived in the city of Carthage, a North African city on the Mediterranean that was a Roman province in 203 A.D. When she was twenty-two years old, Perpetua, a well-educated noblewoman, and her pregnant slave, Felicity, converted to Christianity. Soon after their baptisms, Perpetua was torn from her newborn son, and the two women along with three other Christians were arrested and put in jail. Perpetua kept a diary during their confinement and described the crowded, hot, dark cells, the rough treatment by the guards, and her longing for her infant son. Though her pagan father and even the judge urged her to return to their gods, she refused to relinquish her new faith. She, Felicity, and the other Christians were sentenced to be mauled by wild animals in the amphitheater as part of celebrations for the emperor's birthday. The violent, public death of new mothers: the perfect gift for the emperor who has everything.

Felicity worried that she wouldn't be martyred with the others since it was against the law to kill a pregnant woman. Luckily (… or not?), she gave birth just a few days before the scheduled execution, and a Christian family adopted her baby. The doomed group proceeded gleefully to the amphitheater, singing and shouting to the gathered crowd in praise of God. The crowd, irritated that the Christians were happily facing such a violent death, demanded they be whipped before being fed to the animals. After their scourging, the men were attacked by a leopard, a bear, and a boar, while the women were mauled by a heifer. Though they were all gravely wounded, their deaths eventually came at the hands of soldiers who finished them off with their swords. ✠

PATRON SAINT OF: *cattle; married women*

St. Margaret Clitherow

PLACE OF DEATH	YEAR OF DEATH	MANNER OF DEATH	FEAST DAY
York	*1586 A.D.*	*Squashed under her own front door*	*March 25*

Margaret Clitherow lived (and died) during a complicated time for Catholics in England. When she was born, Catholicism was the state religion; but when Elizabeth I came to power in 1558, all Catholic practices were banned, and compulsory attendance at a Protestant church became the law of the land. Though her family had converted and she had married a practicing Protestant, Margaret returned to Catholicism in her early twenties. Not only did she convert, she raised her children as Catholics and welcomed Catholic priests into her home (in secret) to celebrate Mass. Her brazen displays of faith eventually caught up with her though, and she was arrested and imprisoned along with her servants, whose only crime was remaining faithful to their mistress.

When brought before the local judges, Margaret refused to enter a plea of either guilty or not guilty. This bold step meant that the case couldn't go to a jury trial, which protected her children from being coerced (read: tortured) into testifying against her. That was the good news. The bad news was it also meant she would be automatically sentenced to *peine forte et dure* — that is, "hard and forceful punishment" (or, more plainly, death by crushing). On the morning of her execution, she was stripped, blindfolded, and forced to lie down with a sharp, fist-sized rock under her spine. Then her own front door was placed over her body and piled high with 800 pounds of stones or weights. It took her fifteen minutes to die, but her body was left beneath the door for six hours.

Before her incarceration and painful death by crushing, Margaret and her husband ran a successful butcher shop, which led businesswomen to adopt her as their patron saint. ✠

PATRON SAINT OF: *businesswomen*

St. Stanislaus

PLACE OF DEATH	YEAR OF DEATH	MANNER OF DEATH	FEAST DAY
Krakow	*1079 A.D.*	*Stabbed to death and hacked to pieces*	*April 11*

Though there were no contemporary histories of Stanislaus's life, it's believed he was the only son born to Polish nobles in the village of Szczepanów. He entered the priesthood early in life and quickly became a well-respected spiritual leader in Poland. When the bishop of Krakow died, Stanislaus was elected to take his place, and though he was reluctant to accept the post at first, he did so after Pope Alexander II ordered him to. Once on the job, his leadership style was far from timid. He had, for instance, no trouble clashing with Poland's king, Boleslaw. In the course of a land dispute early in his tenure as bishop, Stanislaus supposedly exhumed a corpse and brought it back to life so that the man could testify in his favor against the king.

After years of battles over Boleslaw's mistreatment of peasants, warmongering, and sexually immoral behavior (which included the kidnapping of a nobleman's wife), Stanislaus took an extreme step: excommunicating the king from the Catholic Church. Getting kicked out of the church was a political disaster for Boleslaw, and he retaliated by accusing Stanislaus of treason. Dispensing of a trial, he sent soldiers to kill Stanislaus, but the men couldn't bring themselves to injure the bishop. Furious, the king took matters into his own hands and killed Stanislaus with a sword while he was performing Mass. The guards then took over and hacked Stanislaus's body to pieces and threw them into a pool outside the church. Despite the rather extreme measures taken to mutilate the corpse, legend has it that the pieces of his body put themselves back together while three eagles soared overhead in protection. The public's outrage at the murder was so total that Boleslaw was forced to flee the country and relinquish his crown. ✳

PATRON SAINT OF: *the city of Krakow; Poland; soldiers in battle*

St. Peter Chanel

PLACE OF DEATH	YEAR OF DEATH	MANNER OF DEATH	FEAST DAY
Futuna	*1840 A.D.*	*Clubbed and cut to pieces*	*April 28*

Peter Chanel, the son of a French peasant farmer, was the first martyr to die in the South Pacific. Though Peter spent many years as a successful parish priest and seminary teacher in France, his dream was to do missionary work. In 1836, he got his wish and was sent with two laymen on a grueling ten-month sea voyage to the tiny island of Futuna, located between Samoa and Fiji.

Their mission was initially welcomed but quickly fell apart. Peter struggled to learn the language, adapt to the local food and customs, and gain the trust of the island's inhabitants.

The mission was looked upon with especial suspicion by Niuliki, an island chieftain and holy man who saw it a threat to his authority. Over the course of three years though, Peter was able to learn the language and won over some of the island's inhabitants with his good works. However, when one of Niuliki's sons, Meitala, asked to be baptized, Niuliki was enraged. The chief ordered warriors to ambush the missionary, club him to death, and cut him into pieces. Unfortunately for Niuliki, the missionary murder was too little, too late. Within the year, almost the entire island of Futuna had converted to Christianity. ✠

PATRON SAINT OF: *Oceania*

St. Florian

PLACE OF DEATH	YEAR OF DEATH	MANNER OF DEATH	FEAST DAY
Enns	*304 A.D.*	*Whipped, flayed, and thrown in a river with a millstone around his neck*	*May 4*

Florian was born around 250 A.D. in what is now Austria, which was then part of the Roman Empire. He joined the Roman army as a teenager and rose quickly to the rank of general. He was also the commander of a firefighting brigade and (according to a very unlikely legend) saved an entire town from fiery destruction with nothing more than a single bucket of water and a prayer. He managed to keep his Christianity secret for years, but reports eventually leaked to the emperor that Florian wasn't enforcing the directives against Christianity in the territory he governed. When Governor Aquilinus came to investigate the charges, Florian immediately confessed his Christianity and refused to save himself by converting.

Florian was first sentenced to die by fire, but he just laughed and said he'd be happy to use the flames to climb to heaven. Thrown by his lack of fear, the soldiers changed course and instead had Florian whipped, flayed, and thrown into the river Enns with a millstone tied around his neck. Florian is still a wildly popular saint in central Europe, where he is closely associated with fire and firefighting. The German prayer to Florian, *O heiliger Sankt Florian, verschon' mein Haus, zünd' and're an*, translates loosely to "Saint Florian, spare my house by setting fire to someone else's." A good prayer to recite as far from your neighbors as possible. ✠

PATRON SAINT OF: *fire; firefighters; brewers; chimney sweeps*

St. Dymphna

PLACE OF DEATH	YEAR OF DEATH	MANNER OF DEATH	FEAST DAY
Geel	*ca. 7th century A.D.*	*Beheaded by her father for refusing to marry him*	*May 15*

Though there's little historical proof of Dymphna's life or death, she was (according to her wildly popular legend) the daughter of an Irish pagan king and a devoutly Christian mother. At fourteen, Dymphna took a vow of chastity, consecrating herself to God. Shortly afterward, her mother passed away, sending Dymphna's father, Damon, into sorrow and a sharp mental decline. When pressed to remarry, Damon insisted he wouldn't until he found a bride as beautiful as his dead wife. Looking around his kingdom, Damon's deranged eye found only one woman as beautiful: his daughter, Dymphna.

When she found out her father was planning to force her into an incestuous marriage, Dymphna supposedly fled with her confessor, Father Gerebernus, on a boat to the continent. They eventually settled in the Belgian town of Geel. There, Dymphna used her wealth to take care of the town's sick and dying. But (no good deed goes unpunished) her extravagant charity only made it easier for her father's agents to track her down. When he finally found them, Damon had Gerebernus killed immediately but tried to coerce Dymphna to come home and marry him. Steady in her faith (and presumably freaked out by her father), she refused. Her enraged father drew his sword and beheaded his fifteen-year-old daughter. Dymphna is frequently depicted in art holding a sword with a devil in chains at her feet. ✠

PATRON SAINT OF: *the emotionally disturbed; runaways; people suffering from mental disorders*

St. Joan of Arc

PLACE OF DEATH	YEAR OF DEATH	MANNER OF DEATH	FEAST DAY
Rouen	*1431 A.D.*	*Burned at the stake after being betrayed by the French king*	*May 30*

Joan of Arc was born in 1412 A.D. to a peasant family in Domrémy, an obscure village in northeastern France remarkable only for its position on a border disputed by England's Henry VI and the presumptive French King Charles. At age twelve, according to the now-famous story (which happened to suit French patriotic interests as well as those of the Catholic Church), Joan began reporting visions of Michael the Archangel, St. Catherine of Alexandria (page 96), and St. Margaret of Antioch (page 60) telling her to find the true king of France and help him regain his throne. In 1428, Joan traveled to Vaucouleurs, a nearby stronghold for Charles, to share her visions and offer her help. Though the sixteen-year-old was ignored at first (no real surprise there), she persisted and was joined by a band of acolytes who believed she was destined to save France. Joan's tenacity eventually paid off, and she was finally given an audience with Charles and convinced him to give her an army to lead to Orléans, then held by the English.

Outfitted in all-white armor, riding high on a white horse, and with her hair cut short like a boy's, Joan led a series of assaults against the English and their allies in France (led by the Duke of Burgundy), driving them across the Loire River. She and her army went behind enemy lines in an aggressive campaign, winning battles along the way and allowing Charles to be properly crowned King Charles VII of France in July of 1429. However, after an unsuccessful run on Paris, her military effectiveness came into question. While defending the town of Compiègne the next spring, she was left outside the town walls when the drawbridge was lifted. Deserted, she was pulled off her horse, taken captive, and sold to the English. The English charged Joan with a litany of crimes, including witchcraft, heresy, and even dressing as a man. Though Charles owed his position to her brave leadership, he refused to help, desiring instead to distance himself from an accused witch. On May 30, 1431, a stake was erected before a crowd in Rouen (then held by the English), and the nineteen-year-old Joan was burned alive at the stake. Twenty years after her death, Charles VII belatedly retried Joan's case, this time finding her not guilty of heresy and clearing her name. ✛

PATRON SAINT OF: *the emotionally disturbed; runaways; people suffering from mental disorders*

St. Erasmus

PLACE OF DEATH	YEAR OF DEATH	MANNER OF DEATH	FEAST DAY
Formiae	*303 A.D.*	*Clubbed, rolled in tar, set on fire, and finally eviscerated*	*June 2*

Though little is known of Erasmus (and his story may be conflated with the legend of another bishop), he is believed to have been the bishop of Formiae, a city just south of Rome. He was forced to flee the city in order to escape the Diocletian persecution, which began in 303 A.D. He survived for a time as a hermit on Mount Lebanon — where he was supposedly kept alive by a raven that brought him food — but he was eventually discovered. The emperor Diocletian threw Erasmus in jail, where he was beaten with clubs, rolled in tar, set on fire, and subjected to many other tortures as well; yet Erasmus somehow endured and remained steadfast in his faith. Legend has it that he was rewarded for his efforts when an angel freed him from captivity, allowing him to go right back to work: performing miracles and converting thousands of pagans to Christianity. But this jubilant period was not to last, and after just one week, he was recaptured. (In Erasmus's Rome, all roads lead to martyrdom.)

Knowing that Erasmus had been impossibly hard to kill in previous punishments, the emperor amended his strategy and sentenced him to an especially gruesome death via mutilation and disembowelment. The executioner cut open the bishop's stomach, pulled out his intestines, nailed one end to a spindle, and then spun that spindle until Erasmus was disemboweled.

Sailors eventually took Erasmus, also known as Elmo, as their patron saint. They saw the blue balls of light sometimes seen at the tops of ships' masts when nearby clouds are electrified as a sign that St. Elmo was protecting them. Over time, this light effect became known as St. Elmo's fire — a relatively peaceful conclusion to this unusually graphic episode (even for a martyr). ✳

PATRON SAINT OF: *sailors; navigators; mariners; those with intestinal disorders, abdominal pain, or stomach diseases*

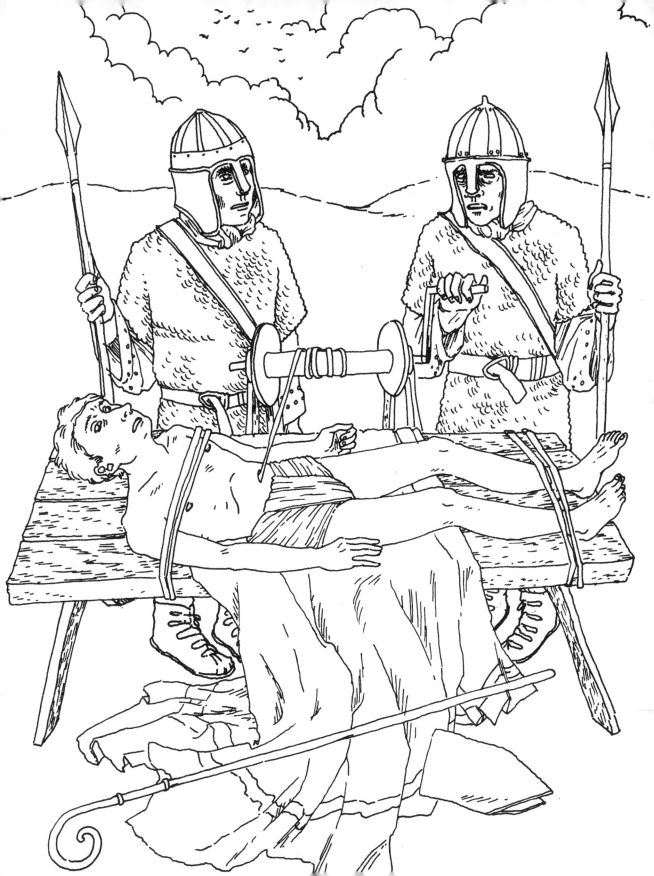

St. Vitus

PLACE OF DEATH	YEAR OF DEATH	MANNER OF DEATH	FEAST DAY
Lucania	303 A.D.	Boiled in a cauldron of oil (or possibly lead and tar)	June 15

There's no historical proof that Vitus even lived (let alone died for his faith), but according to legend, Vitus grew up in Sicily as the son of the pagan senator Hylas. Vitus was secretly introduced to Christianity by his tutor, Modestus, and Modestus's wife and Vitus's nurse, Crescentia. When Hylas found out about his son's conversion, he tried to beat the new religion out of him; and when that didn't work, Hylas had Vitus, Modestus, and Crescentia arrested and brought before the local governor. Though imprisoned and tortured, the devout threesome escaped (supposedly with the help of a friendly angel) to Rome. Once there, Vitus exorcised a demon from Emperor Diocletian's son, but even that rather impressive good deed couldn't keep him free. When it was revealed that Vitus was a Christian, the exorcism was attributed to sorcery, and Modestus, Crescentia, and Vitus were all sent back to jail, this time in Rome.

Every kind of torture was used unsuccessfully on Vitus: Millstones rolled off him harmlessly, and lions rolled over meekly. Finally, all three were thrown into a cauldron of boiling oil (or possibly lead and tar). But when they were on the brink of death, a huge storm blew into the city and knocked down a number of pagan temples, allowing the prisoners to escape to Lucania again with the help of a friendly angel. Unfortunately, they succumbed to their earlier tortures (which perhaps were aided by the boiling oil) a few days later.

As an illustration of how the lives of martyrs can take dramatic turns even after death, Germans in the Middle Ages began dancing on Vitus's feast day, sometimes so fervently that it went on for days and in some cases led to death. Because of this association with fervent dancing and erratic movement, St. Vitus became the patron saint of epilepsy; and the neurological disease chorea — which causes twitching and jerking — became known as St. Vitus's Dance. ✠

PATRON SAINT OF: *dancers; actors; epileptics; Bohemia; people in stormy weather and under threat of animal attacks*

St. Julitta

PLACE OF DEATH	YEAR OF DEATH	MANNER OF DEATH	FEAST DAY
Tarsus	*305 A.D.*	*Scourged, emotionally abused, and beheaded*	*June 16*

According to legend, Julitta was a widowed Christian noblewoman living in Lycaonia (in modern-day Turkey). During the height of the Diocletian persecution, she fled her home with her three-year-old (in some versions, three-month-old) son, Quiriacus, and two maids. They traveled from city to city to evade discovery, but Julitta was recognized in Tarsus (in modern-day south-central Turkey) and brought before Alexander, the region's cruel governor. Seeing her and Quiriacus apprehended, her maids hid and escaped detection. At first, Alexander offered to free Julitta in return for her simply lighting incense as a sacrifice to the pagan gods. When she refused (saying she would rather die than renounce her faith), the judge ordered that she be scourged as an enticement to change her mind. While she was being whipped, the judge held the toddler Quiriacus on his knee, cuddling and attempting to pacify him. Understandably upset at watching his mother tortured, Quiriacus struggled in the judge's lap, crying and scratching the man's face. When his mother cried out, "I am a Christian!" in the middle of her torture, Quiriacus parroted her and said, "I am a Christian!" as well.

Angry at the toddler's quasi-religious outburst, Alexander jumped from his seat and, grabbing Quiriacus by the foot, flung him down the stairs, spattering the steps with blood and brains. Rather than getting upset, Julitta thanked God for making her son a martyr before her and prayed only that she might be granted the same fate. Now beside himself at her stubbornness, Alexander ordered Julitta's sides to be torn with hooks and for boiling pitch to be poured on her feet. Though bystanders begged the grieving mother to light the incense and stop the torture, she insisted she would worship only Jesus and was impatient to meet her son in heaven. Finally the governor decreed that she should be beheaded. A now joyful Julitta was allowed one last prayer, and as she uttered the last word, her head was struck from her body. Both Julitta's and Quiriacus's bodies were taken out of the city and thrown in a mass grave full of dead criminals, but their bodies were later rescued by Julitta's maids and buried in a nearby field. ✠

PATRON SAINT OF: *family happiness; sick children*

St. Alban

PLACE OF DEATH	YEAR OF DEATH	MANNER OF DEATH	FEAST DAY
Verulamium	*304 A.D.*	*Beheaded on a hilltop*	*June 22*

Alban is England's first recorded martyr, despite the fact that he spent most of his life as a pagan. According to legend, Alban's trouble started after he agreed to shelter a priest then on the run from persecution. Alban was so impressed with the priest's behavior that he converted to Christianity in response — but he wasn't able to enjoy his new religion for long. Gossip about the hidden priest eventually reached the government, and soldiers were dispatched to Alban's house. They arrived and found Alban at the door dressed in the priest's clothes, offering himself up for arrest.

When the judge learned that Alban had not only helped the priest escape but had also chosen the new Christian god over the old pagan ones (which Alban called "devils"), the judge ordered him to be whipped. And when Alban *still* refused to revert back to paganism, the judge sentenced him to beheading. On the way to his execution, Alban and his executioners were stopped at a bridge that was blocked by a large crowd that had gathered to watch. Alban, eager for his impending martyrdom, looked up to the sky and prayed, causing the river to run dry and thus allowing the procession to cross its dry bed. Then, feeling thirsty after climbing up the hill he was to be murdered on, Alban prayed again, and a fresh spring rose up for him to drink from.

Alban was now refreshed and ready for death, but these two miracles amazed one of the executioners so much that he begged to be murdered along with Alban. The second executioner happily complied and promptly struck off both of their heads. He wasn't able to enjoy his handiwork for long, however, as retribution immediately followed: he was either struck blind or had his eyes fall out of his head, depending on who's telling the story. Unfortunately, the priest who Alban was protecting, Amphibalus, was captured and stoned to death just a few days later. One might be inclined to think Alban's torture and beheading were for naught, but since we're still reading about him, he might disagree. Alban is frequently depicted in art with a sword, with his miraculous spring, or holding his own severed head. ✠

PATRON SAINT OF: *converts; refugees; torture victims*

St. John the Baptist

PLACE OF DEATH	YEAR OF DEATH	MANNER OF DEATH	FEAST DAY
Machaerus Fortress	*ca. 30 A.D.*	*Head severed and served on a platter*	*June 24*

Very little is known about the early life of John the Baptist, though according to the Gospels, an angel visited John's father prior to John's birth to let him know his son would someday fulfill a religious prophesy. John began his spiritual mission in his early thirties, moving out into the Judea desert (in modern-day southern Israel) to live as a hermit, wearing a camel-hair tunic and eating only honey and locusts. He got "the Baptist" added to his name a few years later when he moved to the banks of the river Jordan to preach and baptize those who came to hear him — including Jesus. After meeting and baptizing Jesus, he became one of his followers and continued to spread Jesus's teachings after his death. John's work was interrupted, however, when his outspoken criticism of King Herod's personal life — especially Herod's marriage to his half brother's wife, Herodias — got him jailed in the Machaerus Fortress, near the Dead Sea.

Even though John was locked up, Herodias continued to nurture a grudge against him and plotted to have him murdered. Herod also wanted to silence John, but he still respected and feared the preacher and didn't want to be responsible for his death. Herodias bided her time and waited for her chance, which came the night of Herod's birthday celebration. She arranged for her fourteen-year-old daughter, Salome, to dance for Herod and his guests. The king enjoyed his stepdaughter's performance so much that he offered her whatever she wanted as a reward — up to half of his kingdom. Coached by her mother, Salome demanded the head of John the Baptist on a platter. Unable to go back on his word, Herod reluctantly complied and dispatched an executioner to the fortress to murder John. After receiving the dismembered head, Salome presented it on a platter to her vindicated mother. Not surprisingly, John the Baptist is frequently depicted in art holding his severed head on a platter. ✠

PATRON SAINT OF: *baptisms; conversions; monastic lives; tailors*

St. Thomas the Apostle

PLACE OF DEATH	YEAR OF DEATH	MANNER OF DEATH	FEAST DAY
Mylapore	*72 A.D.*	*Run through with spears*	*July 3*

Thomas was among Jesus's first apostles, with him through life and at the Last Supper. Beyond these facts, most of Thomas's story is more mythology than history. He received his famous nickname "Doubting Thomas" because at first he didn't believe the other apostles' claim that Jesus had risen from the dead. To convince him, the resurrected Jesus let Thomas put his fingers inside his wounds. With Thomas convinced of his legitimacy, Jesus then instructed his apostles to disperse through the land spreading Christianity. Thomas was assigned a mission in India, but he initially refused to go. Not one to take no for an answer, an apparition of Jesus is then said to have sold Thomas as a slave to the Indian king Gundaphorus, who was looking for a master carpenter at the time. Put in his place, and with the choice taken out of his hands, Thomas changed his mind and left willingly (though a slave) on his mission to India.

In India, Thomas and Gundaphorus worked together to plan a magnificent new palace. The king sent Thomas money regularly, but when he came to inspect his new palace, he learned that Thomas had given the money to the poor and spent his time spreading his religion instead. When he confronted Thomas, the apostle told the king not to worry: the palace was done, but he had built it in heaven, where the king could reside *after* he died. Furious, Gundaphorus threw Thomas in jail.

While the king was planning the best way to kill Thomas, Gundaphorus's brother, Gad, died suddenly. In the afterlife, Gad supposedly saw the heavenly palace Thomas built for his brother. After miraculously returning to life, Gad shared the news with Gundaphorus, and the king and his brother both converted to Christianity. Once released from his bondage, Thomas was free to complete his mission.

Though there are few trustworthy accounts of his travels, he is thought to have traveled the length of India, spreading his gospel and converting others. To this day there's a community on the southwest coast of India who call themselves the "Christians of Saint Thomas." While the date and method of his death are disputed, it's believed that he died in 72 A.D., stabbed with a spear while praying on a hill in Mylapore, on the southern coast of India. ✠

PATRON SAINT OF: *architects; construction workers and other builders; people suffering from blindness; people struggling with doubt*

St. Symphorosa

PLACE OF DEATH	YEAR OF DEATH	MANNER OF DEATH	FEAST DAY
Tibur	*120 A.D.*	*Punched in the face, hung by her hair, and then drowned*	*July 18*

Though the original sources for Symphorosa's and her sons' martyrdoms are in dispute, she supposedly lived with her seven sons in the town of Tibur, just outside of Rome (Tivoli in modern-day Italy). Her husband had been martyred, leaving her a widow, but she lived in peace on a large estate and spent most of her time and money ministering to the poor. But things changed around 120 A.D., when Emperor Hadrian decided Tibur would be a great place for a new palace and temple. When construction was finished and he attempted to make a sacrifice, his gods supposedly sent him a message: Symphorosa and her seven sons had been disrespecting them by flaunting their Christianity, and they wouldn't stand for it any longer. If Hadrian could get them to come and sacrifice to the gods, they'd let him have whatever he wanted.

This seemed like a good deal, so Hadrian had the widow and her sons brought before him for some convincing. But Symphorosa refused to sacrifice to the pagan gods, which she considered to be demons — though she did say that she'd be happy to sacrifice her life (and her sons' lives!) for her *own* god. In a last-ditch effort to convince her, Hadrian had her taken to the Temple of Hercules, where he ordered that she be punched in the face and hung her by her hair. When neither of these techniques had their desired effect, Symphorosa was thrown into a nearby river with a heavy stone tied around her neck. Next up were Symphorosa's seven sons; they also refused to make a sacrifice and were promptly tied to seven stakes, tortured, and killed, each one dying in a different way. One had his throat cut, another was stabbed in the chest, the third was run through the heart with a lance, the fourth was wounded in the back, the fifth in the belly, and the sixth on his sides. The seventh and youngest son was cut in half from top to bottom. After the family's deaths, there was an eighteen-month moratorium on persecutions. (Small consolation.) ✠

PATRON SAINT OF: *Tivoli*

St. Margaret of Antioch

| PLACE OF DEATH | YEAR OF DEATH | MANNER OF DEATH | FEAST DAY |
| Antioch | 304 A.D. | *Escaped from a dragon, fire, and a cauldron of water, only to be beheaded* | July 20 |

The only widely accepted facts about Margaret are that she existed and that she was murdered for her faith. The rest of her wildly popular martyrdom is more than likely fictitious. According to legend, Margaret was born to a pagan prince in Antioch (in modern-day Syria) but was converted to Christianity by her nurse. When her family found out about her conversion, they disowned her. No problem: her nurse adopted her, and Margaret pledged her virginity to God and began work as a shepherdess. Everything was going fine until one day she was spotted by the prefect Olybrius. He was so taken with her good looks that he offered to marry her — but first, she needed to renounce her religion. That wasn't going to happen. When she declined, citing her virginal promise to God as the reason, he sent her to prison.

Margaret was cruelly tortured, beaten with rods, and torn with iron combs. She bled so pro- fusely that Olybrius finally couldn't bear it and had her sent to her prison cell, where Margaret's most outlandish — and most famous — episode took place. In the dark of her cell, the devil appeared to Margaret in the form of a dragon and devoured her. But once inside this dragon-devil, Margaret simply made the sign of the cross, irritating the beast's stomach and causing it to burst open and release her. (Because of her miraculous liberation, Margaret later became the patron saint of another kind of violent bodily escape: pregnancy.) The following day, after refusing again to sacrifice to the pagan gods, Margaret was sentenced to death. She was first tied up and thrown into a fire — but the flames wouldn't touch her. Next, she was dumped into a cauldron of boiling water — but she just stood in the pot, unharmed. Finally, Olybrius ordered her beheaded, which even she couldn't survive. Margaret is frequently depicted in art with a dragon on a chain. ✳

PATRON SAINT OF: *pregnant women; people suffering from sterility*

St. Christina of Bolsena

PLACE OF DEATH	YEAR OF DEATH	MANNER OF DEATH	FEAST DAY
Bolsena	*250 A.D.*	*Tortured, burned, thrown in a lake, and shot through with arrows*	*July 20*

Christina of Bolsena probably existed and was most likely martyred, but her story is largely exaggerated (and frequently conflated with the legend of Christina of Tyre). Christina of Bolsena was the daughter of Urbain, a rich and powerful local judge — and a pagan. Christina converted to Christianity as a young girl and afterward showed little regard for her father's religion. Her teen rebellion went a little too far, however, when she decided to smash her father's gold and silver idols and distribute the precious pieces among the poor. Enraged, her father punished her by beating her with rods and locking her in a dungeon. When she refused to renounce her faith, Urbain (in his capacity as judge) had her publicly torn with hooks, then tied to a rack over a fire. Not only did the teen virgin's body not burn, but the flames also billowed miraculously outward, killing a few bystanders but not Christina.

In his next effort to kill his daughter, Urbain tied a millstone around Christine's neck and threw her into Lake Bolsena. She survived, but her father didn't — he died an agonizing death (from spite!) when he heard that she had lived. Her persecution went on though, because his judicial successor, Dion, had her thrown into a furnace. She spent five days in the flames but still refused to die. Then, like Christina's father, Dion perished unexpectedly. Dion's replacement, Julian, had Christina's tongue and breasts slashed off and then threw her into a cage full of serpents. While she survived these attempts on her life, she became weary of her tortures and prayed for an end to her suffering. When she was taken to the Amphitheater of Bolsena and shot with arrows, she finally passed on, winning the martyrdom she so sorely craved. Christina is frequently depicted in art holding a millstone and standing on a pagan, or holding or being pierced by an arrow. ✠

PATRON SAINT OF: *archers; mariners; millers; Bolsena*

St. Lawrence

PLACE OF DEATH	YEAR OF DEATH	MANNER OF DEATH	FEAST DAY
Rome	*258 A.D.*	*Grilled over open flames*	*August 10*

It's believed that Lawrence was born in Huesca, in what is now northeastern Spain. This also happened to be the home of the future Pope Sixtus II, whom Lawrence met before his rise to power. Together they moved to Rome, and when Sixtus became the Pope in 257 A.D., he made Lawrence, then still in his early twenties, one of the seven deacons of the church. Lawrence was also put in charge of the treasury of the church, which meant that he was responsible for distributing alms to the poor in Rome.

While off fighting Persians in Syria in 258 A.D., the Roman emperor Valerian decided the time was ripe for persecuting Christians back home. He issued a series of edicts requiring Christians to participate in pagan rites and forbidding them from assembling to worship their own god. A few months later, he then ordered all members of the clergy — everyone from low-level priests to the Pope himself — to be executed. Sixtus II and six of his deacons were murdered immediately, but Lawrence was given three days to gather up all of the church's wealth and hand it over to Valerian. Possibly understanding that his fate was sealed either way (according to legend, the Pope had prophesized that Lawrence's martyrdom would closely follow his own), Lawrence decided on a last, grand poke in the eye. On the third day, he showed up with a motley crowd of poor, physically infirm, and otherwise outcast Romans, and proclaimed that they were "the real treasure of the church." Not amused, officials sentenced him on the spot to a slow death roasting on a gridiron over an enormous fire. Despite his suffering, St. Lawrence made a joke of the ordeal, supposedly demanding that his executioners turn him over so he could be cooked evenly on both sides. Lawrence is frequently depicted in art either with or on his gridiron and sometimes surrounded by flames. ✠

PATRON SAINT OF: *cooks and chefs; the poor*

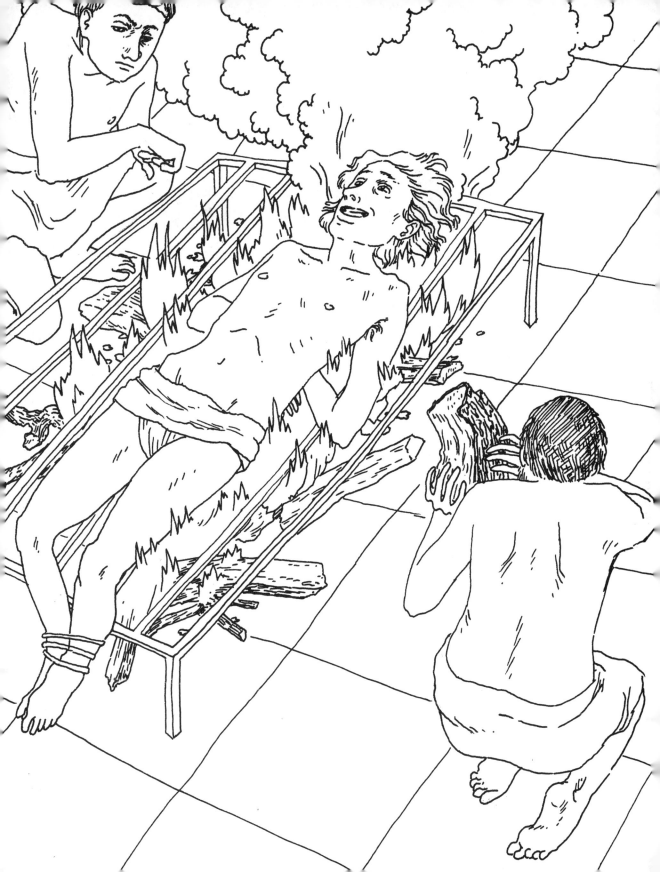

St. Bartholomew

PLACE OF DEATH	YEAR OF DEATH	MANNER OF DEATH	FEAST DAY
Albanopolis	*1ˢᵗ century A.D.*	*Skinned alive and crucified upside down (or beheaded)*	*August 24*

Bartholomew is one the twelve apostles, most likely introduced to Jesus by another apostle, Philip. These are the only facts we know about Bartholomew for sure, but that never keeps a martyr from having a vivid history. Bartholomew was likely born in Galilee, now on the northern edge of Israel. Like all the apostles, Bartholomew was sent on a mission to spread Christianity after Jesus's death. Some traditions have him traveling to India, others to Mesopotamia, Persia, or Ethiopia. Most stories agree that he traveled (and met his end) in Armenia with his fellow apostle Jude.

While in Albanopolis, Armenia, Bartholomew successfully managed to convert the country's king, Polymius. Unfortunately, he only had a short time to celebrate this coup. Polymius's brother, Astyages, wasn't pleased with his brother's conversion and ordered Bartholomew to be killed, slowly and painfully. Astyges supposedly had Bartholomew flayed while still alive. Then he was either beheaded or crucified upside down. Because of his gruesome death, Bartholomew is frequently depicted in art with his muscles exposed and holding a tanner's knife and a strip of skin. Usually the strip of skin is his own, hanging off of his partially flayed body. Quite a bloody legacy to leave. ✷

PATRON SAINT OF: *Armenia; butchers; leather workers; people suffering from nervous diseases and twitching*

St. Genesius

PLACE OF DEATH	YEAR OF DEATH	MANNER OF DEATH	FEAST DAY
Rome	*30 A.D.*	*Tortured and beheaded after an accidental conversion*	*August 25*

An actor, playwright, and the leader of a theatrical troupe (a legendary triple-threat), Genesius is supposed to have lived almost his entire life as a pagan in Rome. Knowing the virulently anti-Christian emperor Diocletian was on his way through town, Genesius planned to curry favor by staging a play mocking Christianity. However, during a scene that featured Genesius in the role of a sick man crying out for baptism, he found himself unexpectedly falling under the sway of the religion he was attempting to lampoon — right in front of Diocletian, no less! Brimming with joy from his newfound faith (and apparently not worried about living much longer), Genesius jumped to the front of the stage and began both praising Jesus and berating the emperor for his brutal persecution of Christians.

Once it became clear that his rant wasn't part of the entertainment, Genesius was promptly arrested. He was burned with torches, beaten with metal rods, stretched on a rack, and torn with metal hooks — but through it all, he refused to renounce his newly acquired faith. When it became clear that he couldn't be tortured into changing his mind, Genesius was beheaded. Though his baptism wasn't strictly legitimate (since the priest performing it was an actor bent on mocking Christianity), Genesius is considered by the church to be "baptized by blood" through his martyrdom. ✠

PATRON SAINT OF: *actors*

St. Moses

PLACE OF DEATH	YEAR OF DEATH	MANNER OF DEATH	FEAST DAY
Skete	*405 A.D.*	*Murdered by Bedouin marauders*	*August 28*

Moses began his life as the slave of an Egyptian official. He was banished from the home of his owner for thievery and under suspicion of murder, and he quickly became the leader of a gang of outlaws that terrorized the Nile Valley. Moses became notorious not only for his string of crimes but for his huge stature and ferocious nature. Once, while on the run from authorities, he hid in the desert outside Alexandria in a monastery in Skete. Impressed by the monks there, he abandoned his life of crime, converted to Christianity, and joined up with the order himself. His transformation was so complete that he was eventually ordained a priest and became the spiritual leader of a colony of hermits.

When Moses was seventy-five, the monks learned that a band of Bedouins planned to attack the colony. The brothers wanted to stay and fight, but Moses, who had become a pacifist, ordered them to retreat to safety instead. Moses, however, stayed in the colony with seven other monks. When the Bedouins arrived, the monks welcomed them and offered them hospitality. In return, the Bedouins robbed and murdered them all. ✠

PATRON SAINT OF: *Africa*

St. Euphemia

PLACE OF DEATH	YEAR OF DEATH	MANNER OF DEATH	FEAST DAY
Chalcedon	*304 A.D.*	*Mauled by a bear*	*September 16*

Though she likely died for her faith, there's little else about Euphemia's story that can be historically verified. According to her legend, she grew up as the daughter of a senator in the city of Chalcedon, across the Bosporus River from modern-day Istanbul. As a beautiful teenager, she disappointed all the men of Chalcedon by proudly declaring that she had consecrated her virginity to the Christian God and wore dark, somber clothes to make sure they got the message.

In the early days of the Diocletian persecution, the governor of Chalcedon decreed that everyone had to offer a sacrifice to Ares, the Roman god of war. When Euphemia refused, she was arrested. Though the youngest of all the Christians arrested, Euphemia was singled out for an especially harsh torture. Luckily she had God on her side, leading to her survival of a series of tortures that relied heavily on the suspension of disbelief. When tied to a burning wheel, for example, she was left unharmed, while the wheel burned away. When shut in a cell with no food and pressed between four large stones, she was fed by a visiting angel, and the stones turned to soft ashes. Finally, Euphemia was thrown into an arena with vicious lions; but instead of attacking her, the lions licked her feet and even wove their tails together to make a seat for her. In the end, however, she met her maker after being either killed by a bear or done in by the sword of a butcher sent in to finish the job. Euphemia is frequently depicted in art with snakes, a tame bear or lion, or (somewhat less pacifically) being stabbed with a sword. ✠

PATRON SAINT OF: *Rovinj, Croatia*

St. Eustace

PLACE OF DEATH	YEAR OF DEATH	MANNER OF DEATH	FEAST DAY
Rome	*118 A.D.*	*Roasted in a bronze bull with his entire family*	*September 20*

Though Eustace (or Eustachius) was supposedly martyred in the second century, his story was probably created out of whole cloth much later on, around the seventh century. True or not, the story of his martyrdom remains popular, especially for its vivid twists and turns. According to legend, before converting to Christianity, Eustace was a Roman general named Placidus, who served under the emperor Trajan. While on a hunting trip in Tivoli, he supposedly encountered a stag with a cross shining brightly between its antlers, accompanied by an image of Jesus. This encounter understandably had a profound effect on him, and he quickly returned home to be baptized into the church, along with the rest of his family. After the conversion, God tested Eustace's faith with an escalating series of catastrophes: Eustace lost his property and position, his servants all died of the plague, his wife was kidnapped and taken aboard a ship, and his two sons were carried off by wild animals during a river crossing.

But throughout his misfortune, Eustace remained strong in his faith, and eventually his family and position were restored to him as a reward. Possibly feeling a little *too* confident at that point, Eustace celebrated by publicly refusing to participate in a pagan sacrifice. That blasphemy didn't escape the notice of then emperor Hadrian, who sentenced Eustace and his family to be mauled by wild lions in the arena. When the lions refused to attack Eustace and his family, Hadrian had a bronze statue of either an ox or a bull brought out and placed over a roaring fire. Once the statue was red-hot, the emperor had the family sealed inside to be roasted alive. Eustace's colorful legend ends with the unsealing of the bronze beast three days after the fire. Though the family was indeed dead, their bodies showed no sign of damage. Not so much as one singed hair. Eustace is frequently depicted in art with a stag or stag's horn (representing his conversion) or with a bull (representing his demise). ✠

PATRON SAINT OF: *hunters; firefighters; people facing adversity*

St. Lorenzo Ruiz

PLACE OF DEATH	YEAR OF DEATH	MANNER OF DEATH	FEAST DAY
Nagasaki	*1637 A.D.*	*Hung upside-down over a pit until he died of suffocation*	*September 28*

Though not part of the clergy, Lorenzo Ruiz is the Philippines' first saint — and the country's first martyr. He was born in Manila in the early seventeenth century and was educated at a school run by Dominican friars. By 1636, Lorenzo was a married father of three, working as a professional calligrapher and clerk for the church. His life seemed prosperous and healthy — until he was accused of murder. The details around the crime and why he was accused are fuzzy, but the charges were most likely false. Fearing a possible death sentence, Lorenzo fled the Philippines on a ship with three Dominican priests, a Japanese priest, and a leper (which also sounds like the introduction to a very unsavory joke).

Unfortunately, they didn't do their homework before leaving shore: they were headed to Japan during a period of extreme Christian persecution. Lorenzo's party stayed briefly with missionaries in Okinawa but were quickly outed as Christians and arrested. Lorenzo and the men were all taken to Nagasaki, where they were tortured for over a year in an attempt to get them to renounce their faith. They all refused. Lorenzo was sentenced to die by a special type of torture called *tsurushi* (or "the pit"), a nearly unbearable torture that was reserved solely for stubborn Christians. At the end of September 1637, Lorenzo was introduced to *tsurushi*: he was bound tightly with ropes and hung upside down from a gallows over a pit. For three days he hung by his feet, the top half of his body swaying in the darkness and stench belowground, before finally dying an agonizing death from suffocation. ✠

PATRON SAINT OF: *the Philippines*

St. Faith

PLACE OF DEATH	YEAR OF DEATH	MANNER OF DEATH	FEAST DAY
Agen	*3rd century A.D.*	*Doused in oil and burned alive on a hot grill*	*October 6*

According to popular but highly suspect legend, the young and beautiful Faith (or Foy) was born to a prominent Christian family in Agen, in the south of France (which was then part of the Roman Empire). Faith had dedicated her life and her virginity to God at a very early age. In fact, her faith was so strong that she is said to have longed for martyrdom. And she got her chance when Decius, the prefect of Rome under Emperor Diocletian, came to visit.

Decius demanded that everyone make sacrifices to the pagan gods or else face torture and death. While most of the town's Christians fled to the countryside to hide, Faith remained in Agen and was one of the first to be arrested.

Faith not only refused to sacrifice to Decius's preferred Roman god (Diana), but she insulted Decius by denouncing the pagan gods as devils. Furious that she would flout his gods so flagrantly, Decius threatened her with every kind of torture. But Faith was up to the challenge. Eager to make her regret her words, Decius had the young virgin bound with iron chains to a brazier, or grill, doused in oil, and roasted over a hot fire. Seeing such a young girl being publicly tortured in such a grotesque way caused the spectators to rise up in protest. Feeling no similar pity for the angry crowd, Decius then had the protesters arrested and beheaded along with the still-smoldering Faith. ✥

PATRON SAINT OF: *pilgrims; prisoners; soldiers*

St. Denis

PLACE OF DEATH	YEAR OF DEATH	MANNER OF DEATH	FEAST DAY
Lutetia	*258 A.D.*	*Stretched on the rack, burned with coals, and decapitated.*	*September 28*

Little is known of Denis's (or Dionysius's) early life except that he was born in what is now Italy and was well respected for his faith and learning. He was sent, along with his less famous martyr friends Rusticus and Eleutherius, as a missionary to Gaul, where the church had been almost wiped out by the persecution of Emperor Decius. The three missionaries settled on an island in the Seine near the city of Lutetia (modern-day Paris) and began preaching and making converts.

In fact, they did such a good job of restoring the church's influence in Lutetia that they attracted the notice of the city's pagan priests. Threatened by the church's resurgence, the priests whipped up public sentiment against the three missionaries and convinced the local authorities to put a stop to their mission, and Denis and his friends were arrested and imprisoned. When they refused to give up their work, they were tortured on the rack and made to lie naked on hot coals. Their executioners also tried to feed the men to wild beasts, but the animals supposedly lay down and refused to eat them. At last, the missionaries were taken to the highest hill in the city (which later got the name Montmartre, or "Mountain of the Martyr," as a result), where they were beheaded with axes. Steadfast in his mission even after death, Denis's body (according to legend, of course) rose, picked up its head, and walked six miles, preaching all the way. (That's dedication.) The Basilica of St. Denis, which later became the burial grounds for the kings of France, was built on the spot where Denis is supposed to have died. St. Denis is frequently depicted with his head in his hands. ✠

PATRON SAINT OF: *France; the city of Paris; possessed people; people suffering from headaches, hydrophobia, or rabies*

St. Ignatius of Antioch

PLACE OF DEATH	YEAR OF DEATH	MANNER OF DEATH	FEAST DAY
Rome	*ca. 108 A.D.*	*Eaten alive by lions in the Coliseum*	*October 17*

A disciple of either John the Evangelist or Peter and Paul, Ignatius served as bishop of Antioch (in modern-day Turkey) for forty years. In 107 A.D., Emperor Trajan passed through Antioch decreeing that all Christians had to choose between their faith or their lives. Ignatius, who had always dreamed of martyrdom, responded to the challenge and was immediately arrested and put on a ship to Rome. Ten soldiers, who he claimed were vicious as leopards, were tasked with guarding Ignatius on the sea voyage. Making good use of his time en route, he wrote seven letters, which became some of the most famous documents of early church theology.

Ignatius's ship reached Rome on December 20, the last day of the public games at the Coliseum. One of the "games" was feeding Christians to lions; the more revered and popular the Christian, the bigger the attraction. So Ignatius was sped through a trial with the prefect and on to the Coliseum so that he could take part. Two lions attacked him at once, fulfilling his dream on the biggest of all possible stages. Ignatius is most famous for being the first to use the term "Catholic Church" in his seven letters. He is frequently depicted in art holding a crucifix and standing between two lions. ✠

PATRON SAINT OF: *the church in the eastern Mediterranean; people suffering from throat diseases*

St. Ursula

PLACE OF DEATH	YEAR OF DEATH	MANNER OF DEATH	FEAST DAY
Cologne	*300–500 A.D.*	*Massacred with 11,000 maidens*	*October 21*

Though Ursula is one of the most popular saints of the Middle Ages, her story may be either the embellished tale of any one of a number of different martyred virgins or possibly completely made up. According to legend, she was an uncommonly beautiful daughter of a British king. Hearing about the royal beauty, a pagan king demanded her hand in marriage for his son. But Ursula was a pious Christian and didn't want to marry a pagan prince — she wanted to remain a virgin. Stalling for time, she asked for and was granted a three-year delay to take a trans-European North Sea voyage to Rome and back.

Ursula, and the ten virgin maidens she chose to accompany her, were each attended by 1,000 maiden (for a total traveling party of over 11,000 people). Near the end of their trip, these eleven ships were driven by a storm to Cologne (in modern-day Germany), where they were met and largely massacred by a Hun army. The king of the Huns gallantly offered to marry Ursula and spare her life, but she refused, and so he shot her dead with an arrow. In 1155 A.D., a mass grave was found in Cologne, which the Catholic Church believed belonged to Ursula and her 11,000 maidens. The Basilica of St. Ursula was built on the ancient site, and a room named the Golden Chamber was added to house the bones, which were arranged in patterns and scenes on the walls and ceilings. Ursula is frequently depicted either with an arrow or being shot with an arrow. Her 11,000 maidens are often pictured in the background being murdered in all sorts of creative ways. ✠

PATRON SAINT OF: *schoolgirls; young women*

St. Jude Thaddeus

PLACE OF DEATH	YEAR OF DEATH	MANNER OF DEATH	FEAST DAY
Persia (probably)	*1st century A.D.*	*Either clubbed and beheaded or cut to pieces, depending on the account*	*October 28*

Though the details of his life are sketchy, Jude was likely Jesus's cousin and definitely one of his original twelve disciples. According to one source, Jude was both a healer and an exorcist, able to cast demons out of pagan idols and leaving the statues crumbling to pieces. After Jesus's death, Jude and another apostle, Simon, left Palestine to spread the gospel throughout the Middle East. In the end, their travels led to their martyrdom. But how exactly Jude was martyred remains a point of some contention: while preaching in Persia, he was either beaten with clubs and beheaded, or cut to pieces with a saw, an axe, or a sickle-shaped sword. An unpleasant end either way.

Jude became associated with desperate situations and impossible causes soon after his death.

Pilgrims who visited his tomb in St. Peter's Basilica in Rome reported episodes in which their problems were resolved in miraculous ways; and two other saints, Bridget and Bernard, both had visions in which God called Jude "the patron saint of the impossible." Despite his early popularity, for centuries Jude was known as the forgotten apostle, partially because his name was so similar to that of Judas, who betrayed Jesus at the Last Supper. Then, in the early dark days of the Great Depression in America, one church on the south side of Chicago revived Jude's story as a means of giving hope to the hopeless. In just a few years, the practice of praying for Jude's help in desperate situations spread across the city and the country, making him one of the most popular saints in the country. Take that, Judas! ✠

PATRON SAINT OF: *hospital workers; hospitals; the Chicago Police Department; also invoked against desperate situations and in regard to hopeless or impossible causes*

St. Ambrose Edward Barlow

PLACE OF DEATH	YEAR OF DEATH	MANNER OF DEATH	FEAST DAY
Lancaster	*1641 A.D.*	*Hanged and torn into pieces (which were then boiled in oil)*	*October 25*

Ambrose Edward Barlow was born outside Manchester, England, in 1585. He was baptized a Catholic, though the religion's practice was illegal at the time. His family finally converted to Protestantism after Ambrose's grandfather died in jail and two-thirds of his father's property was seized as punishment for his beliefs. Ambrose, however, converted back to Catholicism in his early twenties. He was educated in Spain and France, and was ordained a Benedictine monk in 1617. Ambrose then came back to his hometown and worked in secret as the spiritual leader of the countryside's Catholics.

But Ambrose was more outspoken than most Catholic priests, and his secret didn't remain secret for long. He was arrested four times over the next twenty-four years, but he was always released. Then, in March of 1641, the king of England, Charles I, released a proclamation demanding all priests leave the country within a month or else face arrest. On Easter Sunday, Ambrose and his congregation were celebrating Mass when they found themselves surrounded by a Protestant mob led by the local vicar. Though the monk had recently suffered a stroke, he was bound in ropes and taken to Lancaster Castle to stand trial. The trial was predictably brief: Ambrose readily admitted to the crime of being a priest and was sentenced to death. Two days later, he was hanged and dismembered, and for good measure his body parts were all thrown into a cauldron of boiling oil… except, that is, for his head — which was displayed on a pike. ✠

NO PATRONAGE

St. Edmund the King

PLACE OF DEATH	YEAR OF DEATH	MANNER OF DEATH	FEAST DAY
Hone	*ca. 870 A.D.*	*Used as target practice and then decapitated*	*November 20*

Because Vikings decimated Edmund's kingdom and wiped out much of the history of his reign, the details around his life are a little sketchy. It's believed he was crowned king of East Anglia (part of modern-day England) in 855 A.D. at just age fourteen, and he soon gained renown as a just ruler and devout Christian. But in 869, a Viking army attacked and swept through Edmund's land, pillaging every town, monastery, and farm along the way. While some claim Edmund was most likely killed in battle, the more popular, and interesting, version of his legend is that he was captured and then turned over to the Viking chief Ingvar (or Hinguar).

Ingvar told the king he'd spare his life if Edmund would simply renounce his faith and swear to serve the Vikings' purposes instead. When Edmund refused, Ingvar had him beaten with clubs and then tied to a tree and whipped. Angry that Edmund repeatedly called out Jesus's name while being tortured, the Vikings finished Edmund off by shooting him so full of arrows that in death he is said to have resembled a porcupine. For good measure, they also decapitated Edmund and threw his head into the deepest part of the forest. When Edmund's countrymen came to retrieve his remains, they found his body but were stumped as to where his head was. Then, they supposedly heard a voice calling, "Here, here, here," from the forest. Following the voice, they found a tame wolf lying with Edmund's head between its paws. (Vicious animals love protecting saintly body parts.) The wolf allowed the men to take the head and stayed by their side until the king's relics were safely entombed. Edmund is frequently depicted in art in full regalia, holding an arrow or quiver. ✠

PATRON SAINT OF: *wolves; torture victims; various kings; invoked against pandemics*

St. Cecilia

PLACE OF DEATH	YEAR OF DEATH	MANNER OF DEATH	FEAST DAY
Rome	*223 A.D.*	*Beheaded (badly)*	*November 22*

Very little is known about Cecilia (her existence itself is in some doubt), but according to legend, she was born into a historically powerful and noble family in Rome. Though she pledged her virginity to God as a child, she was forced by her family to marry a pagan man named Valerian. On the wedding night, Cecilia told her new husband that there was an angel by her side who would kill him if he ever tried to consummate the marriage. She told him he would be able to see the angel only if he converted to Christianity and was baptized by the Pope. Valerian agreed, and when he returned to Cecilia as a Christian, he supposedly did see the angel by her side. The couple promised to keep their marriage chaste, and the angel rewarded them by crowning the newlyweds with wreaths of roses and lilies.

The newly pious Valerian, along with his converted brother, Tiburtius, began the work of giving Christian burials to all the martyrs killed in Rome. For this, they were quickly arrested and executed by the then provost of Rome, Almachius. Undaunted, Cecilia continued proselytizing, converting 400 pagans before also being arrested and sentenced to be suffocated to death in her own bathhouse. The Romans stoked the flames for a day and a half, but Cecilia didn't so much as break a sweat. Furious, Almachius sent in a soldier to cut off her head. Though the man struck her neck with his sword three times, her head remained attached to her body — for the most part. For three days Cecilia lay bleeding and preaching, converting pilgrims who soaked up her blood with napkins and sponges. (No one said being a martyr was easy.) On the third day, she finally died of blood loss from her half-severed head. In art, Cecilia is frequently depicted surrounded by flowers and musical instruments and wearing a crown. ✶

PATRON SAINT OF: *musicians; composers; singers*

Pope St. Clement I

PLACE OF DEATH	YEAR OF DEATH	MANNER OF DEATH	FEAST DAY
The Black Sea	*99 A.D.*	*Thrown into the Black Sea with an anchor around his neck*	*November 23*

Not much is known about Clement's early life, though it is believed that he was baptized by St. Peter (one of the original apostles) and that he was the fourth Pope. Clement was likely banished from Rome by Emperor Trajan and sent to Crimea to work in the quarries, hauling and cutting stone. He supposedly won thousands of converts in the quarries by miraculously finding a source of water close to where the workers lived. Previously, they had had to walk six miles to get water — and that's a long walk for an imprisoned quarry worker.

Trajan was furious when he heard that Clement was flourishing in his supposed punishment, converting so many that seventy-five churches had to be built to serve them all. To put an end to this conversion rate, Clement was sent to the local prefect who ordered that the Pope be taken by boat to the Black Sea and thrown overboard with an anchor around his neck. According to legend, angels built him a tomb under the sea, and once a year the tide recedes far enough to reveal Clement's resting place. In art, Clement is frequently depicted holding a fish and an anchor or lying in his temple under the sea. ✠

PATRON SAINT OF: *marble workers; boatmen; sailors; lighthouse keepers*

St. Catherine of Alexandria

PLACE OF DEATH	YEAR OF DEATH	MANNER OF DEATH	FEAST DAY
Alexandria	*305 A.D.*	*Beheaded after destroying the spiked wheel meant to tear her apart*	*November 25*

Though likely entirely fictional, Catherine of Alexandria became one of the most popular saints of the Middle Ages and was one of the saints who appeared to Joan of Arc (page 44) in her religious visions. According to legend, Catherine was born to the governor of Alexandria, which was then part of the Roman Empire. She was well educated for a woman of the time and known as a formidable scholar. When she was fourteen, a vision of the Virgin Mary appeared to her, convincing her to convert to Christianity. Just a few years later, Emperor Maxentius began a campaign of persecution against Christians, and Catherine went to him to argue against his cruel assault. Unable to find fault with her airtight reasoning, Maxentius called fifty of his best pagan scholars and philosophers to debate her. Catherine was such an accomplished and devastating orator that not only were they not able to change her mind, many ended up converting — despite the fact that after converting they were, predictably, put to death. Catherine was not someone you'd want to mess with.

Changing tactics, Maxentius offered Catherine his hand in marriage — but only if she denied her faith. She refused, letting him know that both her faith and her virginity belonged to God. Furious that he couldn't defeat her with reason or love, Maxentius had her thrown in prison and beaten with whips. Curious about this young, beautiful genius, both the emperor's wife and the leader of his army visited Catherine in prison, where they were quickly converted and just as quickly martyred. Anxious to contain the spread of converts, Maxentius condemned Catherine to death on a spiked breaking wheel. But as soon as Catherine touched the breaking wheel, it fell miraculously to pieces at her feet. After that, the breaking wheel became known as the Catherine wheel. Maxentius finally had Catherine beheaded, putting an end to her string of conversions. Catherine is frequently depicted in art with her wheel or with a sword. ✠

PATRON SAINT OF: *teachers; students; librarians; craftsmen who work with wheels*

St. Barbara

PLACE OF DEATH	YEAR OF DEATH	MANNER OF DEATH	FEAST DAY
Heliopolis	*311 A.D.*	*Beheaded by her own father*	*December 4*

Though there are no early records of Barbara's martyrdom, her legend was both common and popular by the seventh century. According to her picturesque legend, Barbara lived most of her short life in seclusion, locked away in a tower by her pagan father, Dioscorus. According to different versions of this story, Dioscorus isolated Barbara either to punish her for being disobedient, to hide her beauty from would-be suitors, or just because he was a terrible father. Though he handpicked the servants and teachers who interacted with her, she secretly managed to learn about and eventually convert to Christianity. Soon after Barbara's conversion, Dioscorus embarked on a journey, leaving plans for the construction of a bathhouse on the grounds of their property. Though his plans called for just two windows, Barbara convinced the workmen in his absence to add a third window, symbolizing the Holy Trinity.

When her father came back and saw the changes, Barbara readily divulged the religious motivation behind the third window and admitted to her conversion. He was incensed. Employing some very poor parenting skills, Dioscorus dragged Barbara before the local prefect, who ordered her to be scourged, beaten, and burned until she renounced her faith. Barbara refused, and each night in her cell her wounds were miraculously healed. When she was finally condemned to death, her father cold-bloodedly volunteered to carry out the sentence. However, just as his sword severed her head from her body, he was struck by lightning. Engulfed in flames and reduced to ashes, he perished. Because of her father's timely and satisfying death, Barbara came to be invoked against fire and lightning, later becoming the patron saint of artillery (after it was invented) and other kinds of firepower. Barbara is often depicted in art standing near a tower with three windows. ✠

PATRON SAINT OF: *ammunition workers; artillery; architects; builders; invoked against fire, lightning, explosions, and sudden death*

St. Eulalia

PLACE OF DEATH	YEAR OF DEATH	MANNER OF DEATH	FEAST DAY
Mérida	*304 A.D.*	*Torn with hooks and suffocated*	*December 10*

Eulalia of Mérida likely existed and was martyred for her faith, though the first historical reference to her (a seventh-century hymn) is identical to that regarding another Eulalia, this one from Barcelona. Eulalia of Mérida's story begins with a decree from Emperor Diocletian that all Christians be required to renounce their faith and pledge an oath to Roman gods. To avoid both blasphemy and death, Eulalia's mother fled with her Christian daughter to hide in the Spanish countryside. Though just a tween at the time, Eulalia was very serious (and very vocal) about her faith. Loath to hide her religion even on pain of death, the determined tween escaped from her family in the middle of the night and headed back into Mérida. As soon as the courthouse opened in the morning, she marched in and publicly declared her faith while zealously denouncing the judge for persecuting Christians. To no one's surprise, Eulalia was immediately taken into custody.

Because she was young, beautiful, and rich, the governor of Mérida at first attempted flattery and seduction to get Eulalia to change her mind. If she would simply sacrifice to his gods rather than to hers, he argued, a much easier, torture- and even death-free path lay ahead of her. Instead, she stomped on his idols and spat on his sacrifices. Incensed, the governor ordered the girl to be stripped naked, tortured with metal hooks, and then burned with torches. While the flesh was being torn from her body, Eulalia taunted her torturers by shouting words of thanks and calling each new assault a "trophy of God." The executioners then held fiery torches to her wounds and set her hair on fire. Finally, with her head encased in flames, she died of smoke inhalation. According to her legend, the very moment she died, a dove flew out of her mouth, scaring her executioners so badly that they fled the scene. As they ran away, a snow began to fall, covering Eulalia's naked body and becoming a symbol of her saintliness. Eulalia is typically represented in art with a cross, stake, and dove or, in more risqué paintings and stained glass, as a girl lying naked in the snow. ✠

PATRON SAINT OF: *runaways; torture victims*

St. Lucy

PLACE OF DEATH	YEAR OF DEATH	MANNER OF DEATH	FEAST DAY
Syracuse	304 A.D.	Stabbed in the throat with a sword	December 13

Though Lucy likely lived and died in Syracuse, little else about her story can be verified. (You may not be surprised to hear this when you read how she died.) According to legend, Lucy was born into a wealthy Sicilian family, but things began to unravel before she was out of childhood. Her father died, and her mother, Eutychia, who was filled with anxiety about Lucy's future and chronically ill with a blood disease herself, pledged Lucy in marriage to a pagan named Paschasius. Lucy, meanwhile, had pledged her virginity to God. In order to change her mother's mind, Lucy convinced Eutychia to make a pilgrimage to the tomb of St. Agatha (page 24), where Eutychia's disease was miraculously cured. Thus converted to her daughter's point of view, Eutychia allowed Lucy to break her engagement, remain a virgin, and commit her life to serving the poor and hungry of Syracuse.

Paschasius, unfortunately, wasn't on board with this new plan; and since Sicily was in the thick of the Diocletian persecution at the time, he turned Lucy over the authorities as a Christian. Lucy was sentenced to be defiled in a brothel, but when the guards came to collect her she became so heavy and immovable that even a team of oxen couldn't budge her. Undeterred, the judge ordered Lucy's eyes to be gouged out (in some versions, Lucy plucks her own eyes out to discourage any would-be suitors/rapists). Then he ordered a bonfire to be built around her immobile body. By then they should have realized a simple fire couldn't harm the miraculous, eyeless Lucy. No matter how many times the guards tried to light the fire, and no matter how much oil they poured on it, the fire refused to ignite. In the end, the frustrated guards had to resort to driving a sword through Lucy's young throat.

Lucy, whose name means light, is frequently depicted in art holding her severed eyeballs on a plate or platter. ✛

PATRON SAINT OF: *the blind and those who suffer from other eye maladies; sufferers of hemorrhagic illnesses; laborers; peasants*

St. Anastasia

PLACE OF DEATH	YEAR OF DEATH	MANNER OF DEATH	FEAST DAY
Sirmium	*304 A.D.*	*Crucified, burned, and beheaded*	*December 25*

Little is known about Anastasia beside the fact that she died under the persecution of Diocletian in Sirmium in a Roman province in what is now Serbia. According to legend, Anastasia was born to a noble pagan father and married to a pagan husband, but she was baptized in secret by her mother. She lived her life as a low-key but ardent Christian, devoting her time to helping the poor and other Christians persecuted for their faith. When her husband, Publius, discovered her secret faith, he went from a loving husband to an abusive man. Before leaving on a long trip, he instructed his servants to mistreat her, hinting that no one would get in trouble if she just happened to be dead when he came home. Instead, he was the one who died — possibly in retribution by a still vengeful God looking out for one of his own.

Freed from her husband, Anastasia went back to spending her time ministering to the poor and to those imprisoned for their faith. One day, she visited the jail only to find that all the Christians had been taken away and executed. An officer who found her weeping tried to console her until he realized the reason for her distress: she was a Christian, too. He immediately had her arrested.

Though many tried to get her to abandon her faith (including a local official who was struck blind and later took his own life after making an immodest move on her), Anastasia didn't budge. First, she was locked in a room with no food; but she stubbornly refused to starve to death. Next, she was put on a ship full of prisoners that was designed to sink; but rather than sinking, the ship stayed miraculously afloat and drifted safely back to shore. Duly impressed, the ship's other survivors converted to Christianity — and were then summarily executed for their faith. Anastasia herself was crucified, set on fire, and beheaded. She is frequently depicted in art holding a flame in her hand. ✣

PATRON SAINT OF: *martyrs; weavers; widows*

St. Stephen

PLACE OF DEATH	YEAR OF DEATH	MANNER OF DEATH	FEAST DAY
Jerusalem	*ca. 35 A.D.*	*Stoned to death by a mob after a questionable trial*	*December 26*

Almost nothing is known about Stephen's life before converting to Christianity except that he was born Jewish. After he converted, the twelve apostles chose him as the first deacon of the Christian Church and tasked him with preaching the gospel and distributing food and aid to the poor. He also had the privilege of becoming the church's first martyr. While still alive, Stephen was best known for his special gift as an orator and evangelist. He was happy to enter into theological debate with anyone, leading to an alarming (for the establishment) number of converts in the Jewish community in Jerusalem — some in very high-profile positions.

Stephen's widely successful evangelizing infuriated Jewish leaders, so they laid a plot to stop him. After finding witnesses willing to perjure themselves, they brought Stephen before the supreme rabbinical court in Jerusalem on trumped-up charges of blasphemy against God and Moses. With a heavenly beam of light supposedly shining on his face, Stephen defended himself at length before the court ended his oration, and he insulted the gathered Jews for being too "stiff-necked" to see things his way and convert. The crowd rose up in anger, but Stephen seemed not to notice, exclaiming ecstatically that he saw the sky open up to reveal the recently martyred Jesus in heaven standing beside God and reaching out a hand to him. Adding this blasphemy to the insult against their faith was too much. Without waiting for a verdict, the crowd hauled Stephen out of the court and city and stoned him to death. ✠

PATRON SAINT OF: *stonemasons*

St. Thomas Becket

PLACE OF DEATH	YEAR OF DEATH	MANNER OF DEATH	FEAST DAY
Canterbury	*1170 A.D.*	*Hacked to death by knights in a cathedral*	*December 29*

Born to working-class parents, Thomas showed early signs of both intelligence and ambition. In his early twenties, he began work in the service of Theobald, the archbishop of Canterbury, and before long Theobald was sending him abroad to negotiate important contracts on his behalf. On Theobald's recommendation, King Henry II named Thomas to the powerful post of lord chancellor in 1155. As lord chancellor, Thomas helped the king consolidate his power, even when it hurt the church. Manipulating his post to the king's advantage, the two became very close, and they spent hours together at both work and play. Eventually, the two men came to consider each other brothers. But that all changed after Theobald died and Henry insisted Thomas take his post.

After he became the archbishop of Canterbury, Thomas's demeanor changed completely. Instead of dressing lavishly and hanging out with the king as before, Thomas began fasting and wearing an uncomfortable hair shirt under his clothes as a repudiation of worldly comforts. He also stopped supporting the king's ambitions and began fighting for the rights of the church instead. The once-close friends became such bitter enemies that Thomas had to flee the country in disguise. For years he lived in exile in France while Henry punished Thomas's friends, family, and servants back in England.

Though the two eventually reconciled and the king allowed Thomas to return to England, tempers continued to flare. In a rash moment, Henry supposedly made an angry comment about Thomas, which a group of assembled knights misinterpreted as an order to kill the archbishop. When you're king, people take your whining and complaining very seriously. The knights cornered Thomas in Canterbury Cathedral and attacked him with their swords, spilling his brains onto the stone floor. Henry was distraught when he heard of the murder, realizing it was his careless words that had caused it. He fasted for forty days after Thomas's murder, and years later performed a public penance (which included being whipped at Thomas's tomb) to receive absolution. ✠

PATRON SAINT OF: *the clergy; Exeter College*

Further Reading

BOOKS

- Butler, Alban, Rev. *The Lives of the Fathers, Martyrs, and Other Principal Saints.* Dublin: James
  Duffy, 1866. Bartleby.com, 2010. <http://www.bartleby.com/210/index2.html>.
    *The Lives of the Saints took eighteenth–century English priest Alban Butler thirty years to compile, and
    is considered the most thorough and well-researched compendium of the lives of saints. Butler tried to do
    what few before him attempted: find the truth behind the miracles and monsters, remove additions made
    by romantic transcribers, and right the mistakes of sloppy translators. No wonder it took so long!*

- de Voragine, Jacobus. *The Golden Legend or Lives of the Saints.* 1275. Trans. William Caxton. Ed. F.S.
  Ellis. Temple Classics, 1931. Part of the Internet Medieval Source Book. <http://legacy.fordham.edu/
  halsall/basis/goldenlegend/>.
    Originally compiled by de Voragine around 1260, The Golden Legend *was a blockbuster of the Middle
    Ages — only slightly less popular than the Bible. And this was during a time when copies of books had
    to be handwritten! One of the things that made* The Golden Legend *so popular was how de Voragine
    dispensed almost entirely with accuracy, choosing instead to fill the lives of saints with inspirational
    miracles and fantastical creatures.*

- Foxe, John. *Foxe's Books of Martyrs.* Ed. Harold J. Chadwick. Bridge-Logos, 2001.
    *The Protestant clergyman John Foxe was himself living during a time of persecution in his native
    England while writing his martyrology. Though he included martyrs of the early Church, he concentrated
    (some say a little one-sidedly) on persecutions of his fellow English Protestants — from the sect's inception
    in the fourteenth-century right up through his own lifetime under the Catholic Queen Mary's rule.*

- Guiley, Rosemary Ellen. *The Encyclopedia of Saints.* Checkmark Books, 2001.
    Compiled in the twenty-first-century, Guiley's The Encyclopedia of Saints *is a straightforward and
    (for a modern reader, not well versed in medieval vocabulary) easily digestible collection of the lives and
    deaths of the saints.*

- Ramsgate Benedictine Monks of St. Augustine's Abbey. *The Book of Saints.* 7th ed. A&C Black
  Publishers, 2002.
    First published in 1921, The Book of Saints *compiles the biographies of over 10,000 saints. Because
    it strives for accuracy, the entries tend to be brief and on the dry side.*

WEBSITES:

- *The Catholic Encyclopedia.* <http://www.newadvent.org/cathen/>.
  An encyclopedia of all of the teachings and movements in the Catholic faith, the Catholic Encyclopedia *is notable for including conflicting views and up-to-date scholarship on disputed histories, including the lives and deaths of the martyrs.*

- *Catholic Online.* <http://www.catholic.org/saints/patron.php?>.
  An educational site for Catholics worldwide, Catholic Online *has a database with profiles of over 7,000 saints.*

- *CatholicSaints.Info.* <http://catholicsaints.info/saints-who-were-martyrs/>.
  This site is dedicated to profiles of almost 12,000 Catholic saints.

- *Orthodox Church in America.* <http://oca.org/saints/lives>.
  The official site of the Orthodox Church in America features information about the lives of saints organized by their feast days.